THE OFFICIAL RSPCA PET GUIDE
Care for your
Budgerigar

Tina Hearne

Contents

Acknowledgements

Animal Photography Ltd, Robert Estall, Marc Henrie, Arthur Hissey, Eric Hosking, Frank W. Lane, Pedigree Petfoods Education Centre, Photo Library International, Spectrum, Sue Streeter, ZEFA

Illustrations by Tony Morris

First published 1980
Revised edition 1981
Fourth reprint 1983
Revised edition 1985
9 8 7 6 5

Published by William Collins Sons and Company Limited
London · Glasgow · Sydney · Auckland · Toronto · Johannesburg
© Royal Society for the Prevention of Cruelty to Animals 1980
Printed in Italy by New Interlitho, Milan

ISBN 0 00 410213 4

Collins

Record Card

Record sheet for your own budgerigar

photograph or portrait

Name

Date of birth
(actual or estimated)

Variety   Sex

Colour/description

Feeding notes	Medical record	Breeding record (if applicable)

Veterinary surgeon's name   Surgery hours

Practice address   Tel. no.

Choosing a Budgerigar

The budgerigar is a small species of parrot, native to Australia, where it roves over the semi-arid interior plains in vast flocks. During the last century naturalists introduced the budgerigar into Europe, where its popularity was such that it was soon in great demand. Throughout the nineteenth century nets were laid out on their feeding grounds to catch the wild budgerigars as they came down for seeding grasses. Those which survived being netted, and transported to Europe, were bred in Britain and have become the ancestors of the domestic budgerigar.

For preference it is best to keep budgerigars in an aviary where they may live in a small colony, enjoying freedom of movement and some flight. In the wild they do not build nests, nor will they in captivity (p. 26), but when a selection of nest boxes is provided, the budgerigars will often breed successfully.

Caged budgerigars are much less fortunate, but they are a particularly good pet for a family with very limited space and possibly modest means. If possible, keep a pair of budgerigars in a good sized cage. The essential is that caged birds must be given daily exercise out of the cage. When a budgerigar has to be kept alone it will need the stimulation of appropriate toys, and plenty of human contact. Young budgerigars may learn to talk if they receive lots of encouragement before the age of six months.

Budgerigars are cheerful, hardy companions with more character than one might suppose from their position on the evolutionary scale. Just how much individuality they show depends, as with all pet animals, on the degree of freedom they are allowed, and on the stimulation provided by their surroundings and their companions. The only time fit budgerigars lack vitality is when they are moulting, which seems to be very debilitating for a short while.

The care of budgerigars could hardly be more simple, or undemanding, and it is not surprising that there are thought to be six million of these agreeable little birds in Britain.

Varieties

Light Green budgerigars
The Light Green most resembles the wild type, although about a century or more of intensive breeding has increased its size. The wild Australian budgerigar may be smaller, but it has the similar basic light green colouring, with a yellow mask, shoulders and wings. The six throat spots, the wing and head markings are black.

Although a different colour such as light yellow or dark green will appear from time to time among a flock, the new sport, or mutation, tends to die out in the wild, in favour of the light green, that is genetically dominant.

L. Sky Blue R. Light Green cock

Basic Colour series
In captivity the mutant forms, when they arise, can be bred by skilful enthusiasts, and the variation of form or colour is 'fixed'. Four colour series have arisen: Blue and White, which have a white ground colour; Green and Yellow, which have a yellow ground colour. There are three shades of each colour: light, medium and dark. The three shades of the Blue series, illustrated on the right, are Sky Blue (light); Cobalt (medium); and Mauve (dark). The Whites are known as White Sky Blue (light); White Cobalt (medium); and White Mauve (dark). In the Green series, the succession is: Light Green (light); Dark Green (medium); and Olive Green (dark). Yellows are Light Yellow (light); Dark Yellow (medium); Olive Yellow (dark).

Cobalt cock

Grey, Slate, and Violet factors
In addition to the four basic colour series, three colour factors have arisen that modify the basic colours: the Grey, Slate, and Violet, which also occur in the light, medium, and dark shades. There are, for instance, Grey Greens, Grey Dark Greens, and Grey Olive Greens. The Slate also modifies any of the basic colours slightly.

The Violet factor does not make a bird that colour, except in the case of the Violet Cobalts, but it intensifies their colour.

L. Mauve cock R. Light Green hen

L. Dark Green cock R. Lutino hen

L. Pied Opaline Cobalt R. Grey Green

ky Blue with tufted crest

Albinos and Lutinos

In any natural population of animals an albino form occasionally arises, so lacking in pigmentation that its body colour is pure white, with red eyes. Among budgerigars, the Blue and White series, which have a white ground colour, produce Albino birds. Among the Green and Yellow series, a similar mutation produces an entirely yellow bird with red eyes, known as the Lutino.

Pied budgerigars

The Pied budgerigars are bi-coloured birds, sometimes called Variegateds or Harlequins, with their body colouring broken into sections. Frequently the upper chest is yellow, with a band of green across the lower chest; in the Blue series, the chest will be banded blue and white.

Opaline budgerigars

Ideally there would be no head markings, and the body colour and the ground colour of the wings should correspond. Viewed from behind, an Opaline bird shows a big V of colour between the wings. This area, known as the mantle, should be unmarked.

Crested budgerigars

There are three types of crested budgerigars; those with a flat circular crest, like a Norwich canary; those with a half crest, or fringe; and those with the tufted crest.

Cinnamons and Greywings

In captivity, mutants have arisen with paler wing markings than the normal black, and breeders have used these attractive variants to breed Cinnamons and Greywings.

Cinnamons have a less intense body colour than normal and the head and wing markings and the throat spots are reduced to a light cinnamon brown. Greywings, similarly, possess a genetic factor that reduces all the black markings to light grey, and also reduces the body colour.

Biology

Shape   The streamlined body shape of budgerigars and all birds is, biologically, a necessary adaptation for flight. Breeders value it for aesthetic reasons, and count all the following as faults for exhibition purposes: roach back, pronounced neck, pronounced chest, pronounced paunch, thinness, crossed wing tips, protruding beak, and flattened head.

Feathers   Feathers provide a water-repellent insulation around the body, allowing the budgerigar to maintain a constant temperature. Different feathers, for instance the flights, and down, are adapted for specialized use, and all are attached to muscle for movement. When the feathers are fluffed out a greater volume of air is trapped close to the body for extra warmth. When they lie flat, this volume of air is reduced.

Budgerigars renew their feathers periodically by moulting. Frequent preening keeps the feathers in good condition, and completely restores the structure of those damaged when, as sometimes happens, the interlocking barbules are torn apart.

Temperature   Birds are warm-blooded, or homoiothermic, with a constant body temperature. In the budgerigar this is between 40°C/104°F and 42°C/108°F. To retain body heat, the budgerigar fluffs out its feathers; to lose it, the bird increases its breathing rate above the normal 80–100 per minute, so that heat is lost through expired air. There are no sweat glands through which water may evaporate on the skin surface to reduce body temperature.

Interlocking barbules – magnified.

Toes   Instead of the typical arrangement of three toes forward, and one backward, the budgerigar's toes are paired. One pair is directed forward; the other backward. This is an aid to climbing and is seen in other climbing birds, notably the woodpeckers. The paired arrangement is known as 'zygodactyl', a word derived from the Greek *zugon*, meaning a yoke.

Zygodactyl toes of a climber.

Vent   The vent, or cloaca, is a single opening which is common to the reproductive, digestive and excretory systems. The droppings are a combination of faeces and uric acid crystals, which quickly dry out. In general, birds excrete very little water. Budgerigars, in particular, having evolved in the semi-arid conditions of the Australian outback, do not waste water through excretion.

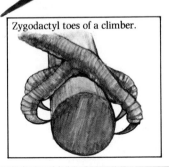

Cere The cere is the exposed, waxy membrane at the base of the beak which is coloured differently according to sex. The word, cere, is derived from the Latin *cera*, meaning wax.

Cock's cere: blue;   hen's cere: brown.

Eyes Birds such as the budgerigar, with eyes set to the sides of the head, have very good sight compared with our own. Our field of vision extends over an angle of about 200°, but only 2° is in sharp focus. Not only is the budgerigar's field of vision much wider, but all the images received, no matter how obliquely, are in sharp focus.

The eyes are protected by three eyelids: the upper, the lower, and the nictitating membrane, which is vestigial in man. The budgerigar, however, can close the third eyelid across the front surface of the eyeball for cleaning, and for protection.

Beak A bird's beak is another adaptation to flight. Heavy jaws and teeth have been replaced by a beak of light-weight keratin. The variation in form is needed to suit very different modes of life and of feeding.

This shape of beak is common to the parrot family, and is particularly well adapted for removing the husks from seed. It is also a considerable aid to climbing, and active budgerigars can often be seen using it as such.

Sometimes the beak is malformed at birth. When the upper mandible is overdeveloped, relative to the lower, the beak is known as 'overshot'. When the lower mandible is overdeveloped, the fault is known as 'undershot'. Veterinary advice should be sought.

Severely undershot beak.

Wings The wings correspond to the fore limbs of other land vertebrates. The large surface area needed for successful adaptation to flight is provided by feathers. These, combined with a very light skeleton, give a big wing area with little increase in weight and minimum loss of body heat.

Aviaries

The most satisfactory way to keep budgerigars is in a well-built aviary with an outside flight area

A well built aviary is the most satisfactory and attractive housing for budgerigars. They are able to live gregariously, as in the wild, enjoying freedom of movement, and some flight, albeit very restricted. They are also free to pair up for breeding, and birds in breeding condition can rear two or three clutches each year. If they are not wanted to breed, it is best to keep only cocks.

A well designed aviary of birds offers the best possible chance of observing their behaviour in captivity.

Basic design
Aviaries vary somewhat in design. The essentials remain the same, however, whether the aviary is free-standing or an extension to the house.

Two compartments are needed: an outdoor flight area, and a weatherproof sleeping area. Budgerigars have proved themselves hardy enough to spend the entire year out of doors in Britain, providing they have some protection from the weather and are safely shut in a ventilated but sheltered roosting-place each night.

onstruction

ie most usual construction is of timber, with wire mesh
 weld mesh screens, and a double door for security. For
eference, the aviary should be built on a concrete apron,
 some similar hard-standing, which is easily sluiced
wn, and rat proof. Even so, one has to remain vigilant,
ice rats can climb the wire mesh and gain access
rough the eaves.

voured aspect

 Britain the aviary should have a south-east or south-
est aspect for adequate warmth and sunshine. A north
cing aviary is too cold and sunless to be suitable.

rnishings

ie sleeping area needs to be furnished with plenty of
rching for the number of birds kept, preferably all of it at
 uniform high level. The budgerigar's preference is
ways for height, and this will prevent jostling for more
voured positions.
 Nesting boxes, when they are provided, may be hung in
e enclosed area, or out in the flight space.
 The flight area will need lots of perching, some under
e protection of the main roof overhang, but not all.
idgerigars sometimes enjoy a soaking in the rain. There
ll also need to be a bird table for food pots. Other
cessories, including the water pots, mineral licks,
ttlefish 'bone', swings, ladders and bunches of seeding
asses can be suspended from the mesh of the wall
reens or roof.

mpatible species

idgerigars must not be kept with small birds such as
naries, which they tend to bully. Compatible species
clude other small members of the parrot family, such as
e cockateels. Weavers and zebra finches have also
oved themselves compatible.

Double security doors   The double doors are a necessary security device to prevent the budgerigars escaping. One door must always be shut before the other is opened, and there must be no space for the birds to fly over the inner door. In this aviary there is a ceiling over the triangle of space defined by the double doors.

Catching aviary birds   Unless an owner spends a great deal of time with his aviary birds, they are unlikely to allow themselves to be handled. Most aviary owners keep a long-handled net for catching their birds should the need arise.

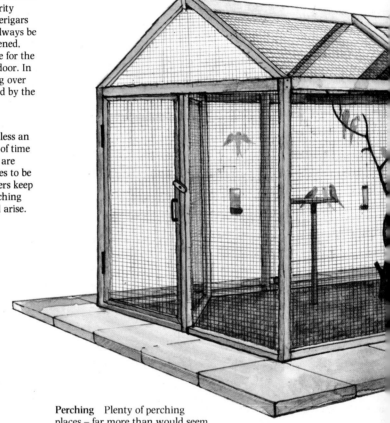

Perching   Plenty of perching places – far more than would seem strictly necessary for the number of birds kept – will be necessary to prevent jostling for favourite positions. We think of budgerigars as extremely docile, but they are capable of being pugnacious with their own kind on occasion. Their particular liking for height should be borne in mind when positioning both perching and nesting boxes.

Bird table   Seed and water hoppers, sprays of seeding grasses and millet are best distributed throughout the aviary, and on the bird table. There will be squabbling unless the birds have room to feed without interference from others.

Roofing Height is important. Budgerigars like to be able to fly and to perch at a good height, and there should be adequate headroom for the keeper to work inside the aviary in comfort.

The sleeping compartment must be strongly roofed, together with part of the outside flight area, to give protection in bad weather.

Sleeping quarters Inside the sleeping quarters the budgerigars must have adequate perching in a dark, draughtproof area, ventilated by an adjustable grille. Budgerigars are hardy enough to withstand winter temperatures in Britain if their sleeping compartment is sturdily built, and frost proof.

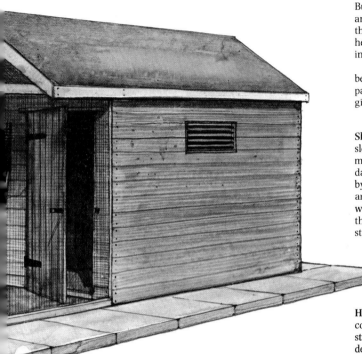

Hard standing The aviary is most conveniently sited on hard standing, which should also be a deterrent to rats. Sometimes rats are attracted to an aviary both by the birds and the presence of their food, and the best aviaries are constructed as rat-proof as possible. Since rats are capable of climbing the wire mesh screens of the flight area, it should not be possible for them to gain access easily at the level of the roof eaves.

Nesting boxes Nesting boxes may be provided from mid-March, either in the sleeping quarters or in the flight area. Provide more boxes than there are pairs of budgerigars, to allow for some choice of site, and position all the boxes at the same height. It is at breeding times that the birds may be quarrelsome, and an odd cock particularly so. An odd hen is unlikely to be difficult: almost certainly one of the cocks would raise two families simultaneously, but he would become exhausted doing so, and it is far better to keep an equal number of cocks and hens.

atchway The budgerigars enter nd leave the sleeping quarters by ay of a hatch, which should be osed in the evening, when they e all roosting, and opened early the morning.

Caging

Housing in cages

Housing budgerigars in a cage is much less satisfactory than in an aviary. As some recompense for cramped conditions the birds will need lots of human contact to which they respond with singing and talking.

Position of cage

The cage should be positioned in a room where the birds will have human contact and yet can be allowed out of the cage in safety. If they show any inclination to fly into the windows these should be screened with light coloured blinds, or netting. Similarly, the door should be hung with a bead, bamboo or net curtain to form a barrier even when it is left open accidentally.

The daily routine should allow for the budgerigars to exercise out of the cage for a while, preferably at times when they are most active, such as the early morning. In many small households, where there is no danger of outside doors being left open, the birds can be left free all day to come and go into their cage as they will.

The cage should not stand in direct sunshine, or in a draught. Many owners find it best to hang the cage on a portable stand that can be repositioned at any time for the comfort of the budgerigar. In the evening it is wise to cover the cage and to take it out of a room where the budgerigars will be distressed by smoke-laden air.

Construction of cage

Choose as large a cage as possible, suitable for housing two budgerigars, with enough room for them to move around it with ease. Manufactured cages are usually made of metal with wire mesh screening. The bars should lie horizontally, to provide a climbing frame.

A home-made budgerigar cage constructed of timber with a wire mesh or weld mesh front, like the breeding cage shown on p. 27 has the advantage of being draught-proof and roomy, and devoid of gimmicky features.

Furnishing the cage

The cage needs to be furnished with perches close to each food and water pot, with a high perch for use at all other times. Bought cages are equipped with dowling perches 1cm/$\frac{1}{2}$in diameter, which are much less satisfactory than a piece of fruit branch which makes a good natural perch. Sand or sandpaper is usually used to line the base of the cage, and ladders, bells, ropes, swings and mirrors are all suitable toys, providing the cage is not over-furnished with them.

Companion budgerigars

Budgerigars which are caged for long periods may become very bored, and the caring owner will have to guard against this. Human contact, suitable toys, and daily exercise will help, but the very best way to keep a budgerigar interested is to provide a companion budgerigar. It is advisable to acquire the budgerigars at the same time and house them together, so that one does not have the chance to become jealous of the other.

A caged bird will need daily exercise, human companionship and a few suitable toys to prevent its becoming bored

Exercise

Physical freedom is very important to the budgerigar. In nature this is a nomadic flock bird, flying immense distances in search of new water holes, seeding grasses and the fresh pastures which spring up very quickly after the thunderstorms which are typical of the area.

The wild budgerigar even embarks on a north-south migration every year, to escape the worst of the summer heat in the northern plains. This entails flying the length of Australia twice every year, and between flights rearing a brood in the eucalyptus scrublands of the south.

It is obvious that in captivity an aviary will give the birds the greatest sense of freedom, and allow for some restricted flight. It is equally obvious that to keep a budgerigar caged permanently, entirely deprived of freedom and its power of flight, shows a complete lack of understanding of the budgerigar's nature and its needs.

It is not difficult to provide caged budgerigars with adequate exercise. If, as suggested on p. 10, they are kept in a room where the windows and doors can be screened, they can be released for at least part of each day. This does not mean that they will fly around restlessly all the time. They are most active in the early morning and at teatime, but during the afternoon will probably settle on a high vantage point and remain quiet for hours.

The budgerigar droppings are very dry, as one would expect from a bird whose natural habitat is a semi-desert region of the world. The droppings will be deposited only at the three or four perching places the bird uses, one of which is bound to be inside its own cage. The other deposits will be left at its chosen vantage points, but the droppings are very easily brushed off.

When birds have been kept caged for generations it is not surprising that their wing muscles begin to atrophy. This accounts for the fact that some budgerigars are weak flyers, and very quickly become exhausted if they escape. Strong birds have been known to establish feral communities in Britain after escaping from confinement.

The RSPCA considers it absolutely wrong to keep a budgerigar permanently caged, no matter how large the cage. These are by nature nomadic birds that rove immense distances in the wild, and in captivity should at least be allowed to exercise out of the cage for a period each day.

Toys help to relieve their boredom but ideally these should be of natural substances such as wood. Budgerigars tend to peck at toys as shown in the photograph, and there is a danger of hollow plastic balls shattering.

Finger-tame budgerigars (below) will allow themselves to be carried back to their cage after exercise, but if the cage door is left open (above) any budgerigar will return to its own perch in time.

Take sensible precautions – such as putting a fire-guard in front of the fireplace, even when there is no fire – to prevent a budgerigar flying up the chimney.

Pied budgerigars *L.* to *R.* Pied White cock; Pied Green cock;
Pied Blue cock; Pied Cobalt cock

Opaline Cinnamon Sky Blue baby hen

Opaline Dark Green hen

Opaline Grey Green cock

Grey cock

Feeding and Watering

Seed mixture

In the wild, budgerigars feed on seeding grasses, which is why they must be fed mixed seed in captivity.

A variety of packeted seed mixes is available. Most are predominantly mixtures of canary seed and millet. The better mixtures are improved by the addition of red rape, linseed, or niger, which are particularly nutritious seeds, with a high fat and protein content. Some mixtures have artificial grains added, with additional nutrients.

Budgerigars also welcome some variety, in the form of sunflower seed and wheat germ, and it is a good practice to hang a bunch of seeding grasses for them.

The budgerigars eat only the kernel of the seed; the husks are always discarded. For this reason owners of caged birds should get into the habit of blowing away the husks that the birds deposit on top of their seed containers. It has been known for budgerigars to starve in a cage where seed was available, hidden by a layer of husks.

Fresh green food

In the wild, budgerigars eat fresh green food as well as seeding grasses. From time to time there are very severe thunderstorms in the Australian interior, and although the land is arid, after a downpour seeds germinate very quickly to produce a lush but short-lived pasture. Budgerigars alight on these pastures to take the green plants, and in captivity will eat chickweed, groundsel, dandelion, and salad greenstuff. Some birds also like a segment of apple or orange; others enjoy grated carrot.

Dietary supplements

Grit is an essential dietary supplement. Seed-eating birds, such as the budgerigar, need the grit to help in the digestion of food in the gizzard. Those deprived of grit will desperately peck at the mortar between bricks and tiles. Although it may not be ideal from a hygienic point of view, it does no other harm if budgerigars peck at the

Budgerigars need to wet their feathers if they are to preen properly. Provide a saucer of tepid water, or a damp turf, early on a warm day, so that the feathers will have time to dry before the temperature falls towards evening.

sandpapers that line their cages. The glues used are non-poisonous and the only danger is if they begin to eat the backing paper.

Cuttlefish 'bone'

Cuttlefish 'bone' is a valuable source of calcium and is a useful tool for young budgerigars to use to trim their beaks. In addition to cuttlefish 'bone', a mineral block, specially formulated for pet animals, should be provided and firmly fixed where the budgerigars can peck at it.

Drinking water

In the wild, budgerigars may have to go several days without drinking. In captivity they may not drink every day, but water must be available and always fresh.

Water for bathing

Water is also needed for bathing. Unless a budgerigar can wet its feathers, it cannot preen properly. This is one reason why budgerigars will sit out in the rain in an aviary.

Those kept in cages must be provided with a shallow saucer of water in which they may splash. Alternatively it is possible to spray budgerigars with luke warm water from an atomizer spray, or to provide them with damp turf to roll on. Provide water for bathing only on warm days, and always allow enough time for the bird's feathers to dry before roosting time.

llet spray

groundsel

chickweed

dandelion

Handling

Caged budgerigars are strong enough to tolerate being handled quite frequently without suffering stress. It is a good idea to accustom them to being handled in the cage for a few days before they are first allowed out for exercise.

If possible, train the budgerigar to become finger-tame, as illustrated, by offering one finger and waiting for the bird to step from its perch onto the proffered hand. Once the budgerigar's trust has been gained in this way it will be possible, with practice, to lift the bird out of the cage on the finger. It is similarly possible to return finger-tame birds to their own perch with no fuss, and without their feathers having been ruffled at all.

Since it clearly takes a great deal of patience and some flair to teach a budgerigar to become finger-tame, there is another method of handling (illustrated below) recommended for the less experienced, and when handling strange budgerigars.

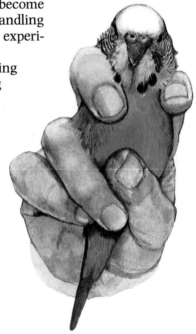

This method is to catch the budgerigar by placing one hand over its back. Allow the tail to lie along the inside of the wrist, and the head to rest between the first and second fingers. The thumb and the other fingers are then free to hold down the wings so that they cannot be fluttered and broken. Once the bird is in position, make a conscious effort to relax the fingers, so that the grip is not too tight.

In an emergency, a budgerigar may be caught by dropping a duster over it. Transport the bird, if necessary, for instance to a veterinary surgeon, either in a box with airholes or in its own cage covered by a cloth.

Talking

A lone budgerigar who enjoys close contact with a patient teacher will very often learn to talk. Cock birds are thought to be more imitative than hen birds, and women are thought better teachers than men, because of their pitch of voice.

The birds need to be encouraged to repeat the sounds they hear while they are still very young. Birds are usually first taught to talk between the ages of five and six weeks, and if they have not succeeded by the age of six months it is doubtful whether they ever will.

Before there can be any hope of success, the teacher must gain the budgerigar's attention. Most experienced handlers first teach the bird to be finger-tame, so that they can talk to it directly, with no distractions, while it perches on one finger, as in the illustration.

The first word to be taught is the budgerigar's own name, which should be chosen because it is short, with a distinctive sound. Later on multi-syllable words and complete phrases may be achieved.

The budgerigar learns to imitate exactly what he hears, and for this reason consistency is essential. The words must always be said with the same accent and inflection, and experienced handlers insist it is best to concentrate on one word at a time. The bird will need to hear each word over and over again, and may not imitate it immediately. As when a young child learns to speak, one may suddenly hear a new word being tried out long after it was last spoken.

Ailments

Scaly face
A grey encrustation that gradually spreads around the beak, cere, eyes, feet, and legs is known as scaly face. It is caused by a minute organism that can be killed off by several applications of a germicidal solution or cream, available on veterinary prescription, or in proprietary form at pet accessory stores and counters.

Scaly face is contagious, and an affected bird must be isolated from all others.

Scaly face with encrustation showing around eyes and cere

Overgrown beak
Budgerigars, and in particular young budgerigars, will trim their own beak on a cuttlefish 'bone', which is also a valuable source of calcium. Sometimes this is not enough to prevent overgrowth, and then regular trimming by a veterinary surgeon will be necessary to control the condition.

Cuttlefish 'bone' is used for beak trimming, and as a source of calcium

Colds, bronchitis, and pneumonia
A mild respiratory disorder may quickly respond to warmth (see hospital cage). If the condition persists, or deteriorates, the bird will need drugs available on veterinary prescription, and any delay in seeking veterinary help may prove fatal.

The advanced symptoms are distressing: the bird sits huddled on its perch, wheezing and gasping for breath with an open beak, and often jerking the tail in a pumping action. Eventually a very sick bird will become too weak even to cling to its own perch.

Hospital cage as used b professional budgerigar breede for sick birds. The light bulb is in separate compartment from th bird, but its heat will warm th cage to 26°C/80°F, which beneficial to ailing budgeriga The thermometer is vital to th equipment: it is dangerous to gue at the temperature, which controlled by switching the lig on and off for perio An ailing budgerigar may w be saved by a handyman quick building a home-made version this ca

Red mite
Red mites are a greyish colour during the day: they take on the red colouring after feeding on their host bird during the night. The mites, which trouble budgerigars less than they trouble canaries, hide in cracks and crevices during the day. Only the most rigorous cleaning, including total immersion of the cage, will eradicate an infestation.

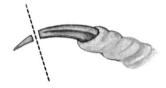

ick budgerigar displaying typical
uddled posture, with feathers
.ffed

straight cut with clippers removes
.e overgrown tip

Sick budgerigars

A sick budgerigar will droop on its perch, quite silent, with feathers fluffed out, and sleeping for much of the time, often with the head tucked under the wing. The vent may become soiled from scouring, and the droppings streaked with blood. Very often the breathing will be affected (see colds, bronchitis, and pneumonia).

It is important to seek veterinary advice early, and to keep the bird in a warm, even temperature.

Overgrown claws

Sometimes a budgerigar's claws will become so overgrown that they will need cutting. Using a pair of animal nail clippers, available at pet accessory stores and counters, cut straight across the overgrown tip of the claw, taking care not to cut into the blood and nerve supply that feeds the nail at its base.

Feather plucking

Budgerigars will sometimes peck and preen their own feathers excessively, due to boredom. The habit, once established, is difficult to stop. The introduction of a mirror, play-objects, or another budgerigar can be beneficial.

Tumours

Growths on or under the skin are common, and have many differing causes. Veterinary advice should be sought in the early stages, since successful treatment is frequently possible.

Regurgitation

The regurgitation of food by healthy budgerigars (p. 28) should not be mistaken for vomiting. In the absence of a mate, or of young, a budgerigar in breeding condition will regurgitate food over a favourite object in its cage, or over its own feet.

The Healthy Budgerigar

Budgerigars are among the hardiest of birds when kept in clean, dry surroundings, and fed good quality food. The most serious disease of the parrot family is psittacosis which is particularly dangerous because it is transmissible to man. Pet birds, unless newly acquired from infected stock, are unlikely to contract it.

It is very difficult for an owner to diagnose illness in a budgerigar because the same symptoms, such as a greenish diarrhoea, appear in more than one complaint including psittacosis. This, and the fact that budgerigar lose condition quickly when ill, makes it imperative to take prompt veterinary advice.

The main signs of health are as follows:

Abdomen	the smooth outline of the bird should be unbroken by hollows, pads of fat, or growths.
Appetite	feeds mostly early morning: dehusks seed with beak and eats only kernels.
Beak	neither undershot or overshot; able to dehusk seed. Gasping with beak open is sign of fever or laboured breathing.
Breathing	quiet and rapid, with beak closed.
Cere	waxy in appearance, with no encrustation. After first moult at about 12 weeks the adult colour shows: blue (male); brown (female).
Claws and feet	no malformation; no encrustation; no overgrown claws.
Demeanour	normally quiet and approachable, with periods of activity. Alert, observant imitative, and acrobatic.
Droppings	firm; quick to harden.
Eyes	bright and watchful; no discharge; third eyelid not showing.
Feathers	luxuriant, with none missing (except at times of moult); well-preened and held close to body except when fluffed out in cold spells or in ill health. A good sheen natural; spiky head feathers a sign of illness.
Forehead	bar-headed birds, with striations across the forehead are young birds not yet flighted.
Stance	sits well clear of the perch, at an angle of 30° from the upright; no hunching huddling; no loss of balance.
Tail	the long tail feathers are lost twice a year during the October and Spring moult
Vent	clean, with no staining or scouring.
Wings	strong, well-feathered, able to support the budgerigar easily in flight.

Life History

Scientific name	*Melopsittacus undulatus*
Incubation period	18 days
Clutch size	3–10
Birth weight	2g
Eyes open	6 days
Plumage complete	28 days
Leave nest	28 days (approx.)
Fully fledged	5–6 weeks
Puberty	3–4 months
Adult weight	35g/1oz–60g/2oz
Best age to breed	males 10+ months females 11+ months
Breeding season	February-September
Retire from breeding	males 6 years females 4 years
Life expectancy	5–10 years

Nest Boxes and Breeding Cages

Budgerigars do not build nests in Australia, nor will they in captivity. In the wild the birds lay their eggs in the hollows of gnarled eucalyptus shrubs, and make no attempt to line the holes, even with plucked feathers.

In captivity budgerigars must be provided with a nesting box, such as the one illustrated here, fitted to the side of a breeding cage. In an aviary there must be a box for each pair of birds, with extra boxes to allow the budgerigars some freedom of choice, and to forestall squabbling.

The depression in the base will hold the eggs, and there is no need to line it or soften it in any way. Essentials are that the nesting box has a small round opening for the hen to use, with a perch beneath it. The cock bird will normally use this perch to feed her while the chicks are in the nest.

The front of the nesting box is fitted with a glass screen behind the wooden door. This allows the interior of the box to be inspected, and the progress of the nestlings noted, without disturbing them or causing them to become chilled.

Droppings accumulate in the nest box very quickly during the month or more the young are developing there. If necessary, it is possible to put the nestlings into a cardboard box temporarily, and remove them to a warm place for a short time while the nest box is being cleaned.

While the clutch is being incubated and reared in the nest box, the cock remains with the family which is dependent on him. The hen leaves her eggs and chicks for only very short periods, but is fed by the cock. The chicks' development is entirely dependent on the cock feeding the hen adequately, so that she, in turn, can feed regurgitated food directly from her beak to her nestlings.

When the young emerge from the nest box, at about four to six weeks, they are again dependent on the cock, who will continue to help feed them while they are slowly learning to dehusk seed for themselves.

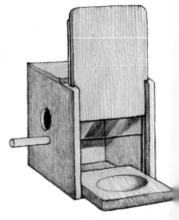

Nesting box opened up to show interior. The saucer-shaped depression serves as a nest. Budgerigars in the wild lay their eggs in hollow trees.

It is a mistake for beginners to provide nest boxes too early in the year. The best time for novice keepers to try to breed their budgerigars is from mid-March to June.

Cage design

Professional budgerigar breeders favour breeding cages of this design, which are stackable and easy to construct.

The design can be recommended just as well for budgerigars that are not breeding. Its simplicity, protection from draughts, and spaciousness are features which many expensive manufactured cages lack.

The cages may be constructed of timber or hardboard, and the wire fronts constructed of weldmesh or wiremesh. Fronts such as the one in the illustration may be bought separately, and fitted to slide into position, or fixed with a separate entrance door for the birds.

Furnishings

The breeding cage does not need furnishing with mirrors or play-objects while a pair of budgerigars is rearing a brood. Boredom is not then a problem, since both cock and hen have a positive role to play. At other times of year, birds kept in a cage of this design will need it furnished as outlined on p. 11.

Nest box

The nest box must not be fixed into position until the birds are in breeding condition (p. 28) and the time of year favourable – usually mid-March to September. Without a nest box this cage provides good accommodation for a pair of birds throughout the year.

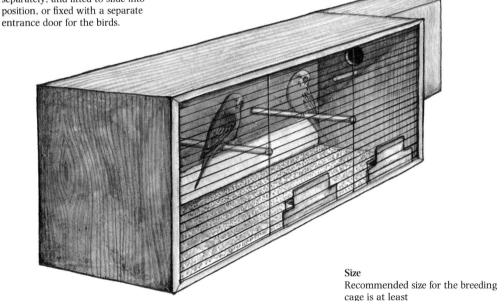

Size

Recommended size for the breeding cage is at least
91 × 45 × 45cm/36 × 18 × 18in.

Reproduction

Breeding condition
Mature budgerigars are likely to reach breeding condition at any time between February and September, and sometimes during the winter too. For novice owners, it is important that the budgerigars should only be provided with nest boxes during the Spring and Summer, when the young chicks will have the best conditions for development.

A cock bird in breeding condition has a very bright blue cere, and a very confident manner. He will pay attention to the hen, and very likely feed her regurgitated food as if she were already incubating her eggs. A hen bird in breeding condition may also regurgitate food, as if for her chicks, and will begin to search for a nesting place.

Clutch size
The normal clutch consists of five or six eggs, with perhaps as many as eight in the first clutch of the year. A good pair of birds may raise three clutches a year, but since this is very exhausting to both the cock and the hen, and produces far more young birds than can be homed satisfactorily, breeding must be controlled.

Three controls are possible: separate the breeding pair; remove the nest box; or remove eggs as they are laid.

Egg laying and incubation
The hen lays her eggs on alternate days, and begins to incubate them from the time the first is laid. For this reason the chicks hatch at intervals after 18 days' incubation.

The hen will hardly leave the nest box during the incubation time, relying on the cock to feed her regurgitated seed. When they hatch, the young in turn will be fed by the hen on regurgitated food and a rich 'crop-milk' that has a high protein content.

The young need no hard food provided for them until they leave the nest and begin to feed on normal mixtures.

airing

lthough many budgerigars are ready for breeding at the
ge of 3–4 months, they are too immature for the strain of
:aring before ten to eleven months old.

A pair normally housed together will usually rear
:veral broods a year, if they are allowed the facilities. In
viaries the birds will pair up by choice, and great care
ust be taken to see there are equal numbers of cocks and
:ns.

Extra nest boxes need to be provided, or there will be
uch squabbling over possession of the most favoured
›xes, which are invariably the highest.

Pair of budgerigars with their
clutch of six young who will not
be ready to leave the nest box until
they are at least four weeks old.
They will then need to spend a
further two weeks with their
parents, until the first difficult task
of learning to de-husk seed has
been learned.

The Young

The chicks spend at least the first four weeks of life in the nest box, tended by both cock and hen, who are devoted in their care of the young.

There are recorded instances of either the cock or the hen dying during the time their young were still in the nest, and yet the surviving parent succeeded in rearing the entire brood. It also happens that if there is a spare hen in a colony of budgerigars, one of the cocks will raise two families, feeding both the hens concerned.

When the chicks hatch they are blind and naked, but by the end of the first week their eyes are open and their feathers beginning to grow. At four weeks they are fully feathered, and will soon leave the protection of the nest.

At this age they need some help in making the transition to hard food, for they find it difficult at first to dehusk the seed. Again the cock helps them, until at six weeks they are fully fledged, able to care for themselves, and ready to be rehomed if necessary. These very young budgerigars have dark horizontal markings across the forehead, which disappear after the first moult at about twelve weeks.

Sexing the young birds is not as easy as sexing adult budgerigars. In good health, adult cocks have a blue or violet cere; adult females have a mushroom brown cere. In many juveniles these colours are not yet distinct and sexing the young becomes a matter of guesswork. This accounts for the fact that many people have given a home to a Joey, only to find later on that he has to be renamed.

Finding homes for budgerigars is not usually so difficult a task as finding homes for many other animals, but it is sensible to allow a breeding pair to raise only a limited number of chicks in a season. This is not only a matter of re-homing: both cock and hen become exhausted by rearing their young, and they should not be expected to raise more than six to eight chicks a year.

The chicks should not be rehomed singly. These are flock birds and a lone budgerigar is never seen in nature.

-month-old hens. *L.* to *R.* Cinnamon Grey, Sky Blue, Grey, Light Green

Index